PEOPLE YOU
SHOULD KNOW

MICHELLE OBAMA

Get to Know the Influential First Lady and Education Advocate

by Lakita Wilson

Consultant:
Katherine Knutson
Professor of Political Science
Gustavus Adolphus College

CAPSTONE PRESS
a capstone imprint

Fact Finders Books are published by Capstone Press, an imprint of Capstone.
1710 Roe Crest Drive, North Mankato, Minnesota 56003
www.capstonepub.com

Library of Congress Cataloging-in-Publication Data is available on the Library of Congress website.
ISBN 978-1-5435-9106-4 (library binding)
ISBN 978-1-4966-6580-5 (paperback)
ISBN 978-1-5435-9107-1 (eBook PDF)

Summary: The first black First Lady in U.S. history (and one of the most beloved), Michelle Obama brought intelligence and passion to her role. Readers will learn how her years as a daughter, student, lawyer, wife, and mother shaped her into the influential education, healthy living, and women's rights advocate she is today.

Image Credits
AP Photo: Charles Dharapak, cover; Dreamstime: Alexandre Fagundes De Fagundes, 14; FDR Presidential Library & Museum: 23 (middle left); Getty Images: Bloomberg/Daniel Acker, 9, Corbis/Harvard University/Joe Wrinn, 12, Darren McCollester, 11; Library of Congress: 23 (bottom left); Newscom: Polaris/Sam Simmonds, 5, Reuters/John Gress, 16, Reuters/Mike Segar, 8, Zuma Press/Ricky Fitchett, 28; Official White House Photo by Chuck Kennedy: 23 (top), 24, 27; Shutterstock: Everett Collection, 21, Faizal Ramli, 29, jdwfoto, 20, Joseph Sohm, 18, JStone, 6, mark reinstein, 23 (middle right), stocklight, 23 (bottom right); U.S. Navy: Photo by Mass Communication Specialist 1st Class Toiete Jackson, 25

Design Elements by Shutterstock

Editorial Credits
Jill Kalz, editor; Kayla Rossow, designer; Svetlana Zhurkin, media researcher;
Tori Abraham, production specialist

Source Notes
page 6, line 3: Lila MacLellan. "How Michelle Obama Handled Falling in Love at Work." https://qz.com/work/1477671/in-becoming-michelle-obama-recalls-falling-in-love-at-work/. Accessed August 2, 2019.
page 6, line 10: The *TODAY* Show. "Michelle Obama on #MeToo: 'Women Are Tired of Being Undervalued.'" https://www.today.com/video/michelle-obama-on-metoo-women-are-tired-of-being-undervalued-1341742147881. Accessed August 2, 2019.
page 7, line 1: Ibid.
page 9, line 13: Michelle Obama. *Becoming*. New York: Crown, an imprint of the Crown Publishing Group, 2018, page 60.
page 10, line 3: Ibid., page 54.
page 10, line 17: Ibid., pages 21–22.
page 12, line 9: Ibid., page 96.
page 16, line 4: Ibid., page 183.
page 20, line 19: Ibid., page 276.
page 20, line 21: Ibid.
page 22, line 8: NBC News. "Michelle Obama: The Historic Legacy of the Nation's First Black First Lady." https://www.nbcnews.com/storyline/president-obama-the-legacy/michelle-obama-historic-legacy-nation-s-first-black-first-lady-n703506. Accessed August 2, 2019.
page 23, line 1: *Becoming*, page 283.
page 28, line 13: Katie Reilly. "Read What Michelle Obama Said in Her Final Remarks as First Lady." *Time Magazine*. http://time.com/4626283/michelle-obama-final-remarks-transcript/. Accessed August 2, 2019.

Printed in the United States of America.
PA99

TABLE OF CONTENTS

Chapter 1
Reaching Girls Globally 4

Chapter 2
Young Michelle 8

Chapter 3
A Political Life 14

Chapter 4
First Lady 22

Glossary 30
Read More 31
Internet Sites 31
Critical Thinking Questions 32
Index 32

1 REACHING GIRLS GLOBALLY

Michelle Obama stood inside the hotel lobby, waiting. She watched for the TV producer to give her the signal. Outside, only a few steps away, a large crowd formed. There was a troop of girls with scouting badges sewn to their vests; women in college T-shirts; a baby wearing bright red headphones over her ears; a girl with curly blond hair standing next to her friend wearing a baseball cap over her hijab; and so many others.

It was October 11, 2018, and the *TODAY* show was welcoming the former First Lady of the United States to the New York City set. When Michelle finally stepped out into the warm, cloudy morning, cheers filled the air. More than 600 women and girls from all around the country clapped and yelled.

Packed bleachers rumbled as people stamped their feet. Girls lunged over the fences with their cell phones, hoping for a selfie. Michelle reached out to high-five a few people as she walked through the crowd. October 11 marked the International Day of the Girl—perfect timing for her big news.

Michelle Obama drew an electric crowd on the set of the *TODAY* show in October 2018.

Long ago, Michelle had written two questions in a purple leather-bound journal.

What kind of person do I want to be?

How do I want to contribute to the world?

Since then, she had been a top lawyer, a college dean, a supportive mom to her two daughters, and a respected First Lady. But now it was time to take her commitment to education worldwide.

"Enough is enough," Michelle told the *TODAY* viewers. "Young women are tired of it. They're tired of being undervalued. They're tired of being disregarded. They're tired of their voices not being invested in and heard." As Michelle's words rang out over the plaza, countless girls, from all kinds of backgrounds, lifted their chins.

Her intelligence, drive, and magnetic personality make Michelle a very effective champion for many causes.

"And if we're going to change that, we have to give them the tools and the skills through education to be able to lift those voices up," Michelle continued.

That morning in New York City, Michelle announced her newest education **initiative**, the Global Girls Alliance. The huge project may have come as a surprise to some people. But Michelle Obama had been preparing for it her entire life.

The Global Girls Alliance

The Global Girls Alliance is now called the Girls Opportunity Alliance. Michelle Obama and the Obama Foundation started this initiative to empower girls all around the world through education. The foundation helps community organizations set up funds to pay for girls' education. It also teaches young people across the country about the importance of education and how to get involved.

initiative—a program to raise awareness for a social cause

Michelle Obama was born Michelle Robinson on January 17, 1964. Her parents, Fraser and Marian, lived on the upper floor of a little brick house in Chicago, Illinois. There they raised Michelle and her older brother, Craig.

Michelle's brother, Craig, appeared with her during Barack Obama's presidential run in 2008.

The neighborhood was middle class and mixed race. Family was always nearby—an aunt and uncle owned the house and lived downstairs. Family gatherings were common at Michelle's grandfather's house just around the corner.

Michelle's mother taught her how to read at a young age. Her father taught her about jazz, art, and basketball. Michelle was driven to be the best student from the first day of school. She skipped second grade and entered gifted classes by sixth grade. Her parents wanted her and her brother to do well. "We were their investment, me and Craig," she said later. "Everything went into us."

Michelle went to high school at Whitney M. Young, a brand-new school designed to bring in smart kids of all races. Getting there involved "ninety minutes of nerve-pummeling travel on two different city bus routes as well as a transfer downtown." Michelle left her house at 5:00 a.m. and got home between 6:00 and 7:00 p.m.

She worried about not standing out among the 1,900 other students. She worked hard to be a good student. She took advanced classes, earned good grades, and served on the student council.

Her hard work led to acceptance at Princeton University in New Jersey. In the summer of 1981, she moved to campus. She discovered she was a definite **minority** at the school. "Princeton was extremely white and extremely male," she wrote. "Black students made up less than 9 percent of my freshman class." But Michelle also knew that being at the top of her class was the way to get ahead.

After Princeton, Michelle applied to the best law schools in the country. She went to Harvard Law School in Cambridge, Massachusetts. In 1988, she earned a job as a lawyer at one of the top law firms in Chicago.

Michelle spent many long hours in Langdell Hall, home to the Harvard Law School library.

minority—a group that makes up less than half of a large group

Michelle's future husband, Barack Obama, in 1990

Michelle was a first-year lawyer when she was asked to **mentor** a Harvard law student over the summer named Barack Obama. He was three years older than Michelle and said to be very talented. At first, Michelle was not impressed. "I'd checked out his photo," Michelle said. "A less-than-flattering, poorly lit headshot of a guy with a big smile and a whiff of geekiness." He was also late to their first meeting.

DID YOU KNOW?

Barack Obama also attended Harvard Law School. He proposed to Michelle the same day he took the **bar exam** to become a lawyer.

It didn't take long for him to win her over, though. Barack was smart and confident. The two became close friends. Eventually they both realized they weren't interested in other people. They married on October 3, 1992. Their wedding song was Stevie Wonder's "You and I (We Can Conquer the World)," a big hint at what was to come.

The Value of Life

Michelle's friend Suzanne Alele died of cancer in 1990. Michelle's father died the next year. Their passing made Michelle rethink her life. She realized that she didn't enjoy being a lawyer, even though she was very good at it. She felt there was more she could offer the world through a different kind of career.

bar exam—a test a person must pass to practice law
mentor—to act as an adviser or teacher

A POLITICAL LIFE

Shortly before the wedding, Michelle left her law job to work in the mayor's office. She worked as a **liaison** between the city's many departments. Her coworkers Susan Sher and Valerie Jarrett greatly influenced her. They showed her how to speak her mind, to be confident in her choices, and to balance her personal and work lives.

Michelle worked in Chicago's City Hall building in the early 1990s.

In 1993, Michelle was hired to be the leader of a group called Public Allies. Their goal was to **recruit** young people and give them the skills needed for public service. The students would be the next generation of community leaders.

During that time, Barack had been working at a law firm, teaching law classes, and writing a book about his life. Then he had the opportunity to run for a seat in the Illinois state **legislature**.

The Written Word

To help her collect her thoughts, Michelle bought a purple journal. She wrote about things she was interested in, her unhappiness as a lawyer, and her worries about the future.

legislature—a group of people who make or change laws
liaison—someone who helps two groups to connect and understand each other
recruit—to sign someone up for something

Michelle didn't think it was a good idea for her husband to become a state senator. She didn't like what she had seen from many politicians. "Most of what I knew about state politics came from what I read in the newspaper, and none of it seemed especially good or productive," she said. But in the end, she said yes, and Barack was elected.

As Barack began a new role in politics, Michelle began a new job as a leader at the University of Chicago. The job allowed her to get students involved with the city. It also had another benefit—better health insurance for starting a family. Malia was born in 1998 and Sasha in 2001.

The Obamas (Sasha, Michelle, Barack, and Malia) in 2004

In 1999, Barack decided to run for the
U.S. House of Representatives. He lost that
election, but in 2004, he ran for a seat in the
U.S. Senate. This time he won—by the largest
margin in Illinois state history. Michelle was
also busy during this time, taking a new job as
a leader at the University of Chicago hospital.

What's What?

State senators are elected by voters from
a district in their state and work in the state
legislature. U.S. senators are elected by
voters in their state and work in Congress in
Washington, D.C. Voters in a state elect two
U.S. senators to represent them. Voters also
elect one person to represent them in the
U.S. House of Representatives. The number
of U.S. representatives serving each state
depends upon a state's population.

While Barack worked in Washington, D.C., Michelle cared for their daughters and worked hard. She was promoted to a more notable job at the University of Chicago hospital, helping the hospital connect to the local community.

Although Barack had been in office only a few years, people started to ask if he would run for president in 2008. The choice was up to Michelle. She agreed. On February 10, 2007, Barack announced his candidacy. A few months later, Michelle decided to spend less time working at the hospital so she could spend more time **campaigning** for Barack.

Michelle and her daughters joined Barack on the 2008 presidential campaign trail whenever possible.

Barack was used to being in the spotlight. However, now the light was on Michelle too. Reporters told her she didn't smile enough. Her words were twisted to make her sound bad. Some critics called her names. They even picked on her clothes and the way she looked.

Michelle told funny stories about Barack leaving the butter out or forgetting to pick up his socks. She thought the stories would help people see the Obamas as a "normal" family. But some people said she was trying to embarrass her husband. A TV interview with the whole family was picked apart by viewers around the country. Michelle got her first taste of how mean the public could be. She didn't like it.

Michelle decided to try something different. She began talking about things that were most important to her: her husband and children, education, and her Chicago roots.

campaign—to get people to vote for a certain person or to support an idea

After a shaky start, Michelle found her voice on the campaign trail and captured voters' attention.

She also listened. Voters told her about their lives and their problems. Michelle vowed that she would help. Those people began to take notice. They felt like she heard their words.

On November 4, 2008, Michelle went to a Chicago elementary school and cast her vote for the next president.

That night, before the results were in, she had her own final words for her husband. "I'm proud of you, no matter what happens," she told him. "You've done so much good."

"So have you," he reminded her. "We've both done all right."

At exactly 10:00 p.m., the news arrived. Barack Obama would become the forty-fourth president of the United States of America.

The night of November 4, 2008, Barack's supporters celebrated the Obamas as the next First Family of the United States.

The 2008 Election

Barack Obama's running mate was Joe Biden, a senator from Delaware. They were up against Arizona senator John McCain and his running mate, Alaska governor Sarah Palin. More than 131 million people voted. It was the highest voter turnout percentage for a presidential race in 40 years.

4 > FIRST LADY

The Obamas had only a few months to prepare for the move to Washington, D.C. Sasha and Malia needed to be signed up for new schools. Michelle would need to hire a staff and begin to plan major White House events, such as formal dinners and cultural performances. People often asked Michelle what kind of First Lady she would be. "I won't know until I get there," she replied.

DID YOU KNOW?

Michelle's mother, Marian Robinson, made the journey to Washington, D.C., with the family. Marian tried to stay out of the spotlight during her eight years living in the White House. She turned down Secret Service protection and did her own laundry and shopping.

First Ladies

"There is no handbook for incoming First Ladies," Michelle wrote. "It's not technically a job, nor is it an official title. It comes with no salary and no spelled-out set of obligations." Throughout the years, First Ladies have taken on many different roles when they lived at the White House.

- Martha Washington did not enjoy politics, but she was well known for supporting U.S. soldiers.

- Eleanor Roosevelt was a strong **advocate** for women, people who were poor, and minorities.

- Nancy Reagan fought against drug and alcohol abuse.

- Laura Bush, a librarian, promoted education and developed programs to help teach children how to read.

Martha Washington

Eleanor Roosevelt

Nancy Reagan

Laura Bush

advocate—a person who supports an idea or plan

During Barack's campaign, Michelle talked with families all across the country. Now, as First Lady, she was in a position to help them. She learned how challenging life could be for military families. They moved a lot. Spouses had to find new jobs. Children had to adjust to new schools. Military members could be sent out on duty for a year or more, which could affect the families they left behind. It could be hard for **veterans** to switch from the military to everyday life. Injuries taken in the line of duty could be life changing.

As First Lady, Michelle didn't shy away from openly expressing her feelings on issues about which she was passionate.

In 2011, the First Lady worked with Dr. Jill Biden, the vice president's wife, to start Joining Forces. This initiative raised awareness and provided support for service members, veterans, and their families.

Michelle brought her message of support to military families across the country.

Secret Codes

The job of the Secret Service is to protect important government officials, including the president and his or her family. Each member of the First Family is given a code name. Barack was "Renegade." Michelle was "Renaissance." Sasha and Malia chose "Rosebud" and "Radiance."

veteran—a former member of the military

As First Lady, Michelle spent some time traveling. During Barack's two presidential **terms**, she made more than 20 trips abroad. While Barack met with foreign leaders, Michelle spoke to everyday people.

She spoke to kids about the challenges she faced in her early life. She gave speeches about race and gender inequality. She supported art education and encouraged students to go to college.

She also worked on problems in the United States. Childhood obesity was getting worse. In 2009, Michelle and a group of students planted a vegetable garden at the White House to encourage people to eat healthy. Michelle campaigned for the passage of the Healthy, Hunger-Free Kids Act. This law said that schools had to provide more fresh, healthy foods to their students.

DID YOU KNOW?

On November 6, 2012, Barack Obama was reelected to a second term as U.S. president.

The next year, Michelle started Let's Move! The campaign encouraged children to get up and move through exercise and dancing. The First Lady sang about healthy foods on *Sesame Street*. She rapped about fresh vegetables on YouTube. She Hula-Hooped on the White House lawn.

Michelle turned her words about fitness into action with local students outside the White House in 2011.

term—a set period of time that elected leaders serve in office

While in the White House, Michelle's main goal was to keep her daughters' lives private. After years of Barack working and traveling far from home, the whole family was finally together under one roof. Michelle's staff knew that her daughters' events came first on her schedule. Malia and Sasha, who were 10 and 7 years old when they moved into the White House, did chores and had a regular bedtime.

On January 6, 2017, Michelle spoke to the nation as the First Lady for the last time. Her words were meant especially for the youth of America. "I want our young people to know that they matter, that they belong," she said. "Lead by example with hope, never fear. And know that I will be with you, rooting for you and working to support you for the rest of my life."

Surrounded by educators, Michelle gave an uplifting, hope-filled final speech as First Lady.

In November 2018, Michelle's memoir, *Becoming*, was published. It sold 725,000 copies its first day and more than 10 million copies in the first six months. It seemed that people had missed her inspiring words and wanted more.

The title of Michelle's memoir implies not a destination, but an ongoing journey toward the best you can be.

Obama Media

Michelle and Barack Obama created their own production company in 2018. Higher Ground, in partnership with Netflix, creates series and movies that promote understanding between people. It also works with Spotify to create an assortment of podcasts that inform, entertain, and inspire.

GLOSSARY

advocate (AD-vuh-kuht)—a person who supports an idea or plan

bar exam (BAR ig-zam)—a test a person must pass to practice law

campaign (kam-PAYN)—to get people to vote for a certain person or to support an idea

initiative (i-NISH-eh-tihv)—a program to raise awareness for a social cause

legislature (LEJ-eh-slay-chur)—a group of people who make or change laws

liaison (lee-AY-zahn)—someone who helps two groups to connect and understand each other

mentor (MEN-tur)—to act as an adviser or teacher

minority (meh-NOR-uh-tee)—a group that makes up less than half of a large group

recruit (reh-KROOT)—to sign someone up for something

term (TERM)—a set period of time that elected leaders serve in office

veteran (VEH-teh-rehn)—a former member of the military

READ MORE

Lucidon, Amanda. *Reach Higher: An Inspiring Photo Celebration of First Lady Michelle Obama.* New York: Crown Books for Young Readers, 2018.

Rajczak Nelson, Kristen. *Michelle Obama: First Lady, Author, and Activist.* New York: Lucent Press, 2020.

Strand, Jennifer. *Michelle Obama.* Minneapolis: ABDO Zoom, 2018.

INTERNET SITES

Britannica Kids: Michelle Obama
https://kids.britannica.com/kids/article/Michelle-Obama/574555

Kiddle Encyclopedia: Michelle Obama Facts for Kids
https://kids.kiddle.co/Michelle_Obama

Let's Move!
https://letsmove.obamawhitehouse.archives.gov/kids

CRITICAL THINKING QUESTIONS

1. Michelle once wrote two questions to herself in a purple journal (see page 6). How would you answer those questions for her today?

2. Through initiatives such as the Girls Opportunity Alliance and Let's Move!, Michelle has become a powerful education advocate. Why do you think education is so important to Michelle? How does education help people?

3. In what ways do you identify with Michelle? In what ways do you not? Use details from the text to explain your answers.

INDEX

2008 presidential election, 20–21

Alele, Suzanne, 13

Becoming, 29
Biden, Jill, 25
Biden, Joe, 21
Bush, Laura, 23

campaigning, 18–20, 24
childhood, 8–10
code names, First Family's, 25

early jobs, 11–12, 14–15, 16, 17
education, 6, 7, 19, 23, 26
education, Michelle's, 9–11

First Ladies, former, 23
First Lady, 22, 23, 24–28

Girls Opportunity Alliance, 7
Global Girls Alliance, 7

Harvard Law School, 11, 12
Healthy, Hunger-Free Kids Act, 26
Higher Ground production company, 29

Joining Forces, 25

lawyer, 6, 11, 12, 13, 15
Let's Move!, 27

marriage, 13
McCain, John, 21
military veterans, 24–25

Obama, Barack (husband), 12–13, 15–19, 19–20, 24, 25, 26, 28, 29
Obama, Malia (daughter), 6, 16, 18, 19, 22, 25, 28
Obama, Sasha (daughter), 6, 16, 18, 19, 22, 25, 28

Palin, Sarah, 21
politics, 15–28
Princeton University, 10–11
Public Allies, 15

Reagan, Nancy, 23
Robinson, Craig (brother), 8, 9
Robinson, Fraser (father), 8, 9, 13
Robinson, Marian (mother), 8, 9, 22
Roosevelt, Eleanor, 23

Secret Service, 22, 25

TODAY, 4–7

University of Chicago, 16, 17, 18

Washington, Martha, 23
White House, 22, 23, 27, 28
Wonder, Stevie, 13